NOTES

TO MY

SON

Notes to My Son
Published by Sharknado Press
Lakewood, CO

ISBN: 978-1-7333816-0-4

FAMILY & RELATIONSHIPS / Parenting / Fatherhood
FAMILY & RELATIONSHIPS / Life Stages / General

Cover Design by Natasha Brown
Interior Design by Victoria Wolf
Back Cover Photo by Donna McCoy

QUANTITY PURCHASES: Schools, companies, professional groups, clubs, and other organizations may qualify for special terms when ordering quantities of this title. For information, email info@sharknadopress.com.

To my loving wife Ashley and son Summit. My life tastes so much better with you in it.

Table of Contents

INTRODUCTION.. 1

NOTE 1.. 9
Honor Your Commitments

NOTE 2... 13
Every Day Counts

NOTE 3... 17
Live in the Present, Learn from the Past, and Love Your Future

NOTE 4... 21
H.A.L.T.

NOTE 5... 25
Hold Us Accountable for the "Why"

NOTE 6... 29
Make Success a Habit

NOTE 7... 33
Words = Wisdom (Or at Least the Pathway to It)

NOTE 8... 37
Daydreams May Create Your Future

NOTE 9... 41
Compete to Complete

NOTE 10.. 45
Hope Is Out of Your Control; Action Is in Your Influence and Purview

NOTE 11.. 49
Experience Can Be Expensive or Cheap

NOTE 12.. 53
Diversity of Thought

NOTE 13.. 57
Don't Become an Ideologue Without Being Fully Informed

NOTE 14... 61
Your Parents Will Make Mistakes; Jot Them Down
and Reference Them Later

NOTE 15... 65
Nothing Is Taboo

NOTE 16... 69
Father vs. Dad

NOTE 17... 73
Selfishly Selfless

NOTE 18... 77
Once You Post, It's Out There Forever

NOTE 19... 81
Financial Literacy

NOTE 20... 85
Psychology vs. Physiology: Different yet Dynamically Relevant

NOTE 21... 89
Cognitive Dissonance

NOTE 22... 93
Never Stop Learning . . . and Applying

NOTE 23... 97
Once a Man, Twice a Child

NOTE 24... 101
When in Doubt, Be Nice

NOTE 25... 105
Work Hard, Think Harder . . .

EPILOGUE 113

ACKNOWLEDGMENTS 117

ABOUT THE AUTHOR 121

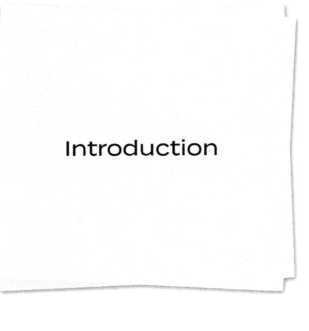

Introduction

I am not certain there is anything more intimidating than the daunting role of being a father

As we get closer to your birth date when we will finally hold you in our arms, I can tell you my emotions imitate a roller coaster. It's both exhilarating and exhausting at the same time. The fact that my fingerprints will be all over your upbringing brings about my inner competitive desire to be the best damn father ever, along with the ever-present thought of failure as a possible outcome. Such is life. I decided to write these notes to you to be transparent. To let you glimpse both the vulnerability and fragility of thought as you come into this world. Your mother and I just want to do you a solid (to use a term from my generation). We want to make sure we give you the right advice at the right time. While this is a Utopian mindset, we are also realists. We will be imperfect; we will give inappropriate advice; we will get emotional when we should be equanimous. At our core, though, we want to be fair, loving, and supportive parents.

I've received so much advice already from books, classes, friends, teachers and even strangers in elevators (yep, it happens everywhere). I'm just waiting for a neighbor in an airport stall next to me to give me sage fatherly advice. That's about the only portion of my inhabited planet where advice has yet to be bestowed. Don't get me wrong. I am a listener and so appreciative of any two cents that people impart upon me. You never know when the gold will rise from the pyrite. In the end, though, I have to take that advice and craft the valuable parts into the mold from which we will raise you. You are a snowflake: diverse and unique to all other human beings. While you may share our DNA, you are you. An individual designed to make an imprint on this world. Our role is to give you multiple pathways. The path you decide to take is ultimately up to you. We will be there when you fall, when you need an ear and when you just need a high-five or an old reliable bear hug. Your life is yours to live. We will love you no matter what life you decide to lead.

I can't tell you the exact moment I wanted to be a father. I can tell you there was a time when this wasn't the case. You'll find life takes you on different tangents and you can decide to decline a tangent and formulate your own ride or remain on course. I was in my late thirties when my mindset changed. Your cousin was a culprit in the turn. As he grew, so did my inner fire to be a father. I have always said if the burning desire to be a father doesn't reside within you, don't do it. We've got too many fathers as it is who aren't dads. (See that topic later.) There should be confidence, not conceitedness, in this decision. There should be humility, not haughtiness, that pushes this desire to realization. What allowed me to pursue this ultimate responsibility and adventure were my failures. The more I failed, the more I learned. The more I learned, the more confident I became in finding solutions to the iceberg-sized problems that rise up and confront us as we're cruising through life.

I still find the prospect of fatherhood so full of hubris. Who am I to think I can impart the infinite wisdom to another impressionable human being? Your mom is a key catalyst in this. I am so lucky to have a partner who is so eager to be a mother. What she lacks in experience she more than makes up for in research. Her strength (as you've already found as you continue your free ride in her belly) is without equal. Her persistence unmatched. Frankly, she inspires me to ratchet up my game.

I can't wait to have these conversations with you face to face. Writing is a bit one-sided and unfair, as my audience cannot yet respond. But I look forward to the time when you can and you will. I will be wrong more than I'm right, but just know the conversations will be authentic. These thoughts are not gospel; they are just coming from your old man's point of view. I have developed and will continue to lean on unconscious bias. Good or bad, we are programmed every day based on our experiences. We may achieve self-awareness and ultimately self-actualization with avid discipline. I battle this every single day. Being self-aware calls biases to the top and thus acknowledges their existence in the calculation. I spell this out to state clearly that these are my thoughts. They are simply meant to place you at the starting gates of complex concepts. How you finish the race is entirely up to you. See you soon . . . my son.

P.S. I love you so much and I haven't even met you. . . . How is that even possible?

Note
1

Honor Your Commitments

There's a reason I am placing this one first. Commitments equal your credibility. Your credibility is your brand. Your brand is invaluable.

In China, they've started a "social score." This measures your commitment to honor societal norms. That's a bit extreme in my opinion, but the theory isn't all that far out. Even if we aren't publicly tracking social scores in America, you better believe those around you are tracking your social score. We may live in an "ish" world now, but it doesn't mean you have to. In the financial credit world, we are measured quantitatively through a FICO score. This is an attempt to validate whether or not you are worthy of repaying a debt. This is most widely used by banks that are vetting you on a mortgage/ auto/business loan. I'd rather you focus on your perceived ATHCA (Ability To Honor Commitments Always) score. You may say it's impossible to honor all commitments for the rest of your life. Maybe. However, if you pause, take a breath and think about each commitment before you give confirmation, you can protect your ability to honor a large majority of them. Saying no sometimes is better than saying yes. Only say yes to what you can hold true to. This will enhance your brand both personally and professionally. You are the master of your ability and only you can say what you can achieve. Master this and your relationships will be full of honor, respect, and trust.

"Be that person who keeps their word; who honors their commitments even when it's not convenient."

—Lucy MacDonald

Note

2

Every Day Counts

Each of us gets a max of 365 days a year, and if we're lucky and live past eighty, we may get over 29,000 of them.

Every day counts. Even if it's a day of rest and relaxation, make it count. Soon you'll look back and wonder what happened to them, and why they are flying by. How can you squeeze a bit more value out of each day? How do you "Suck out all the marrow of life?" as Henry David Thoreau wrote in Walden, and as quoted in one of my favorite films, Dead Poet's Society? You get no recalls on time. Trust me, I've tried. At 11:59 p.m., you can't snap your fingers and roll back to 5:30 a.m. We can't turn back time . . . regardless of what Cher says. Who's Cher? We'll sing the song together someday.

The best advice I can give you is to treat every single day as if it's your last. How would you think differently? Would your behavior change? Would you smile at that stranger instead of frowning? Would you finally stop and pet that cute golden lab you keep passing on the sidewalk? Might you call your mother one or two extra times that day just to check in and tell her you love her? Perhaps we would finally take that father/son trip we've been talking about. Perhaps today is the day you muster the ten seconds of courage to ask out that pulchritudinous blonde in your science class. And by the way, yep, I actually look forward to the birds and the bees conversation, which we've probably already had by now if you're reading this book. I hope it was memorable. I hope it was fun. I hope it wasn't gross. I hope you follow my advice! Your mom and I decided before you were born that I would own that one.

Every day is a new adventure. Ask me sometime about my 5:00 a.m. wake-up calls for fishing expeditions in the local pond. And yes, the fish will get bigger and bigger each time I tell the tale…

"I really do think about the fact that every day counts. I believe that every individual counts, and so I believe that every day counts and I try not to waste it."

— Madeleine Albright

Note
3

Live in the Present,
Learn from the Past, and
Love Your Future

The purpose of the past is to remind us of previous decisions. This is important, but not imperative to thriving.

Your future is somewhat in your control and somewhat out of your control. Let me explain. To increase your confidence in a future with a high degree of financial and mental well-being, it's important to have goals and to execute actions to reach your goals. You can influence your future; however, you cannot control it.

Focus on the now. What you see, hear, and touch today is under your greatest degree of influence. Days are fleeting, as we just discussed in Note 2, but moments are experienced and remembered. This is part of making each day count. I plan on living in every moment possible with you.

I purposely battle with balancing the present and the future. My constant struggle is in asking myself this question: "If I stop and smell the roses, how do I know there will be flowers in my family's future?" I don't have the perfect answer, but I do have the persistence to persevere in these moments. Right or wrong, you will be the catalyst of the present for me. I want no regrets on time lost. I want the same for you. As you grow up (and I know you will do so in the blink of an eye), I want you to notice. I hope you can minimize those mindless moments, like driving the car for twenty-five miles on autopilot, not even remembering if you changed lanes. Instead, I hope you enjoy the mindset that's able to pause the moment, rewind, and fast forward at your own discretion, and DVR that instance to become a memory to recall tomorrow.

"The true way to live is to enjoy every moment as it passes, and surely it is in the everyday things around us that the beauty of life lies."

—Laura Ingalls Wilder

Note
4

H.A.L.T.

One of my mentors gave me this acronym. The principle is simple; the execution much more difficult.

H = Hungry
A = Angry
L = Lonely
T = Tired

Never make a key decision in one of these states of being. Each state causes degradation in your ability to rationalize clearly. If you are hungry, your physiology is saying it needs nourishment. Listen and feed it. If you are angry or lonely, the limbic part of your brain (more on this later) is potentially going to push you in an irrational direction. If you are fatigued, again, your body is in a state of unrest and this must be quenched prior to thinking clearly.

Lean into each of these states, absorb the pain, take the appropriate action to diffuse it (eat, calm down, grab a dance partner, sleep) ,and then make your decision. I promise this technique will save many relationships, both professionally and personally.

"Don't make a permanent

decision based on

a temporary emotion."

—Author Unknown

Note
5

Hold Us Accountable for the "Why"

Whenever I speak to a new hire who joins our company, I extend two pieces of advice. The first is to be patient with their education.

When you try to consume too much at once, the law of diminishing returns kicks in, and you'll have data leakage. Education should be in digestible bites so you can retain it enough to apply it. The second piece of advice I give is to lean in early and often with their voice. With no historical bias, they have no preconceived notions of what works, so their voice of questioning and input is extra valuable.

You can ensure you are doing this by asking "why" . . . a lot. I expect new hires to ask why at least two hundred times during their first ninety days. I expect to hear "Why?" from you at least a thousand times before you are old enough to live on your own. The true magic exists when you are able to ask yourself why without being prompted. Disrupting yourself (meaning changing your status quo) is a technique that you can apply to both your personal and professional life.

You can't find the why unless you are humble. Humility acknowledges the fact that you don't have all the answers. I personally use this as a gauge for hubris. If there's someone in my sphere of influence who never seems to ask a question and instead always seems to have the answer, I know that humility went on holiday for this person. The only way to truly get an answer is to ask questions. And if you ask enough of them, the answers will eventually present themselves to you.

We will practice the concept of radical transparency with you. What is "RT"? It's when I give you an answer to a question even when I know it's gonna hurt. It's leading a conversation with honesty front and center even when strong emotions may be the reaction from it. I can promise we will not be perfect in our execution, but our mindset will be to live it. We will ask you to reciprocate back to us. Honesty is the foundation of trust. And trust equals love. I promise you our love will be there. Just ask me why . . .

"You get what you tolerate."

—Henry Cloud

Note
6

Make Success
a Habit

Success is a vague word. So let's unvague it. Success means what you want it to mean.

Simply put, success means achieving a goal you set out to achieve. For example, let's say Father Time wins (always does) and you gain weight, so you set a goal to drop ten pounds. Once you achieve that goal, you have obtained success. That's an empirical, clear example. But what about a less clear goal, such as, "I want to be an even better person"? That's a bit ambiguous, so we'll need to quantify what that means. We could add many metrics to the calculation that could ultimately determine success. Do we let more people enter the lane in front of us from an on-ramp? Do we give up our seats to a woman in fatigues to honor her service? Do we help an elderly man cross the road? Do we give more of our time and capital to our favorite charity? Do we volunteer for the school PTA? Do we become a mentor in the Big Brothers Big Sisters program? Do we smile more? Do we offer our assistance to a friend in need? Do we volunteer for an overseas assignment in the Peace Corps? I could go on and on.

Here's the key, though: success is your own definition. Thus, you determine what success means for you. In business, your bosses, shareholders, peers and other constituents may tell you what goals you are to obtain. They cannot, however, dictate what success is for you. That is yours and yours alone to manage.

Success should be stretched. Push yourself and always reach for more, but make sure it's attainable. If you want to hike a fourteener (which you will on my back at an early age), you will need to train for it. Does success mean finishing a goal, or does it include the time it takes to complete it? Perhaps you want to become more spiritual. Meditation may be the pathway to that goal. What is success, though? Is it to meditate once a month, once a week, daily . . . ? For how long? You are the conductor of your cause. You decide what success looks like.

My only advice is to make it a habit. Second place does not receive a true reward in this world. Regardless of our culture shifting to "everyone gets a trophy," this mentality still does not pay the bills. It only fosters mediocrity. If you want the ability to make better choices financially and emotionally, practice success daily. It can be small victories, such as becoming more patient with your spouse (present company included), or larger wins, such as starting your own business. By making success a habit, your body, mind, and soul become used to it and success then becomes a subconscious expectation. You become programmed to win.

"We become what

we repeatedly do."

—Sean Covey

Note
7

Words = Wisdom (Or at
Least the Pathway to It)

Words can be daggers to the heart, or they can lift it. Words can demotivate an employee or they can inspire her to burst through the ceiling.

Words can cause a riot or they can create peace. Words can unfairly win an election or they can cause a societal enhancement. Words can kill an idea or they can land a man on the moon. Words can end a relationship or begin a new one, such as, "Will you be my wife?"

Words demand respect from those who spew them and those responsible to listen. Words are to be respected. Don't use or treat them lightly. They matter. Everything we say or do matters. Action, you'll find, exists throughout these notes. Words are especially important because they linger. They may not be tangible, but they are certainly lasting. Once uttered, they cannot be taken back. They are fingerprints scribed into the circuitry boards of your audience. Make sure those prints have a positive impact.

Words can be beautiful. Elocution is a highly regarded skill set that truly separates leaders in our society. If you don't aspire to be a leader, no worries, as the power of words applies to you no matter your chosen vocation. They are relevant in all relationships. Become an active listener, and you will enhance your vocabulary. Become a voracious reader and adopt new and valuable vernacular.

Your tonality matters too. Words have different context depending on the tone in which they are received. In Mandarin Chinese, for example, the word "Ba" can have four different meanings depending on how it is pronounced. Mind your tone.

Non-verbal reactions and actions are most certainly language as well and powerfully convey a message. Sometimes, non-verbal language conflicts with the words. In this case, the deliverer may be struggling to be authentic. Let your radar ring true and be cautious in this case.

A former CEO of mine once gave me sage advice. He said, "You are always onstage, Eric." Meaning, no matter what, you are being watched. Own your language at all times, as you wouldn't want it to be misunderstood.

Effective communication is extremely hard to achieve. Becoming an avid student of language, will make the challenge much less daunting.

"The single biggest problem in communication is the illusion that it has taken place."

—George Bernard Shaw

Note
8

Daydreams May Create Your Future

I admit it. I'm a dreamer. I don't like to think with barriers, even though unconscious biases and barriers do exist for me.

I constantly have to chisel barriers out of my thoughts. If we think without barriers, there truly may be less in our way.

Barriers exist in many forms: money, naysayers, time, network, geography, state of being, etc. Some are easy to knock down; others require dynamite. Celebrate your daydreams. Ideally, they will be moral, legal, ethical and do no harm to your family. If you want to be an actor, dream it, and do your damndest to live it. We will support you. If you want to be an astronaut, dream it and give it your all to achieve it. We will support you. If you want to be the president of the United States (I may give you a sanity test for this one), dream it and haul ass to get there. We will support you.

Nothing is out of your reach unless you allow the barriers to stop you. Many obstacles will move in front of you, but you can find creative ways to surmount them. Non-dreamers will continue to try and stop you. They will only be bumps in the road that only slightly slow you down. Your destination is of your own volition. I cannot wait to see where you wind up . . .

"It's not just a daydream if you

decide to make it your life."

—"*She's on Fire*"

by Train

Note
9

Compete
to Complete

I believe in completion, not perfection. You'll hear the term "paralysis by analysis" on occasion. It means we get stuck by data.

Too many options, scenarios, variables, or other unknowns that debilitate us from being able to move. Complete the task; don't perfect it.

No one has the ideal definition of perfect. You'll find that life is full of metrics. Metrics are objectives or goals you wish to attain, or that others tell you to attain. You've probably heard the statement, "Anything worth doing, is worth doing right." I couldn't agree more. However, right could mean different things to different audiences. For example, personally, you may have a goal of running a marathon. This demands a daily discipline in preparation. Unless you are extremely gifted, you can't just wake up one day and decide, "Yep, the sun's out and there just happens to be a race in town. I'm gonna run 26.2 miles today." You'll have to train for it. Now, the tasks are pretty straightforward: lace up your shoes, hit the starting gates, and then finish 26.2 miles on foot at some point. So where's the gray? How much you train, how fast you run, and how long it takes to finish the race are all your choices.

Compete to complete. A professional example would be a revenue goal of 8 percent year-over-year growth. Your boss or board give you a goal, but the activities and decisions it takes to get there are your call. You may make mistakes along the way. These are just stepping stones to a greater tomorrow. The only true failure is when you don't learn from the failure. You may choose to target a new customer demographic to achieve your growth. You may focus on re-attracting former customers. You may grow wallet share with existing customers. I can promise you as long as your pathway to achieving 8 percent growth is moral, ethical, and legal, your boss won't care how you did it.

By accelerating your completion percentage on tasks, you can complete more tasks. This does not mean you half-ass anything. Deliver the product as if your mother were the recipient. Well . . . perhaps that's a bad simile as your mother will have a personal bias to your success. Present it to the mayor of your town. Is it sufficient or do you need more time?

Lean Six Sigma includes two concepts known as accuracy and precision. Accuracy is hitting the same area repeatedly (consistently). Precision is hitting the target you are aiming for, but perhaps less consistently in placement. Ideally, one would hit the target with both accuracy and precision, but if I have to choose one over the other, I prefer accuracy: being consistent and true to your vision and subsequent objectives, but knowing that completion is paramount. Finish that book you are reading, finish the race you trained for, finish your obligations to your friends and family, finish that last drop of water in your bottle (shout out to your mom here) and, most importantly finish for YOU! No one owns your accountability but you.

"Seek to complete rather

than compete."

—Linda Burton

Note
10

Hope Is Out of Your
Control; Action Is in Your
Influence and Purview

Hope is a very, very powerful word. Just watch a movie, or a show, or read a fiction book.

Hope is the ultimate catalyst for both aspirational and inspirational motivations. It conjures up the most inner circuits of our limbic brain. Many scientists would argue this is one of the variables that separates us from other species. Hope, however, is not in our control. I encourage you to be cautious of words such as "I hope," "I think," or even "I believe." These words relinquish your ability to influence, and more importantly, control a path forward. I've heard these terms used as excuses to not perform well, both professionally and personally. They become people-made barriers that should be malleable, yet they are treated as rigid.

Whether or not you are working with peers, friends, or family, stay in a positive partner zone. This means keeping the conversation quantifiable with facts and tangible data over hyperbole. Now, I absolutely get that the term "belief" is at the essence of organized religion. This is not the same connotation of belief I am speaking of here. The context I am referring to is circumstantial and encompasses many situations. For example:

"I hope the pilot knows what she is doing today, but I am not in control." You could validate her flight hours prior to selecting that route. I wonder why most people don't.

"I hope my doctor knows what he is doing." Of course, you can get a second and third opinion if you choose. (You are in control.)

"I hope I win the lottery." No hope here; you won't.

"I hope I find my true love." To find love, you must be searching for it. Love won't show up with a knock on the front door. Seek and you shall find. (You are in control.)

Hope and belief are siblings. They both galvanize en masse. Clusters of humanity are formed around these concepts. They both feel very good, our L-dopa is tipping off the scales as the hope pistons fire in our brains and bodies. Belief brings us to tears as we aspire to be inspired. I can relate more closely to karma.

Karma is based on our actions and the ripple effects of those actions on others. The cause and effect is a result of what we do vs. what we believe. The lower your karmic debt, the more you've given to those around you.

I prefer to think of "beliefs" as foundational tenets or core values to who I am. What conceptually intangible beliefs do I value most in this world that include tangible actions? Loyalty, integrity, fidelity, health, and humility are all beliefs that I hold dear, as I control them. There is no passing the buck on these core principles, as I own the outcomes. I not only influence, but I also 100 percent dictate the outcomes. Own your actions in life. Even in reactions, you still mandate the results. No one else can answer for you.

Decide, dictate and deliver on your own fate.

"Everything you do comes

back to you."

—Author Unknown

Note
11

Experience Can
Be Expensive
or Cheap

Failures are merely a pathway to success. The only true failure is not performing a postmortem on what you learned from the event.

The school of hard knocks is definitely not for everyone, but I know you will be prepared for it. I failed miserably when the US economy crashed in 2008. I had thirteen rental properties that all went belly up when several of the mortgages adjusted. What did I learn?

1) Make your money on the front end when you buy. If you don't hedge with some built-in equity when you buy, you have already lost. Don't put yourself in a position where you hope appreciation happens. Make it happen.

2) I did not neutralize the ambiguity of the investment. When you go fixed on a mortgage (even when it's higher), you can predict and thus execute on a precise budget for your investment property. I purchased with a floating mortgage on the seconds, and it put the investments underwater.

3) Patience was not a virtue I subscribed to. You should look at over a hundred investments

before you buy. I looked at twenty. There are always deals to be had. You just have to remain resolute in finding the right one.

That was a very expensive lesson. Sometimes the lessons and thus experiences come much more cheaply. My greatest teachers were some of the worst leaders. Why? Because I learned what not to do. Dysfunction is much easier to see than function. (Side note: The 5 Dysfunctions of a Team is a fantastic book.) Ego infects your ability to treat people with respect, listen to good advice, and solve true problems. These teachers taught me the value of humility by not showing it. I saw the impact of those around them. No one wants to follow a know-it-all.

One way I can quickly identify an inflated ego is by a simple observation. If someone never asks a question, they are arrogant. Or if they actually ask a question, but don't really listen to your answer and instead give you their solution, these people are even worse. Some of them are self-aware and others are not. You will need to deal with these people professionally, but you can decide to exclude them from your personal circle. They are prevalent. I know I keep beating the humility drum and I will not apologize for it. If you are not humble, you cannot listen. If you won't listen, you will not hear the better solutions literally smacking you in the face.

"Experience is a school the

lessons of which are very expensive,

but it's the only school where

you can learn something valuable."

—Benjamin Franklin

Note
12

Diversity
of Thought

It troubles me greatly that we attribute diversity to tangible characteristics of race, ethnicity, age, sexual preference, and origin.

It isn't these titles that frustrate me. It's that it still doesn't capture the true power behind the term diversity. Each of us brings a culmination of our life experience. Call it baggage, failures, wins, episodes, events or decisions. This calculation of our core being is what makes us truly unique.

Do race, ethnicity, age, sexual preference and origin play potential roles in shaping our lives? Absolutely! However, they are supporting actors, not the lead role. A high degree of emotional intelligence is required to fully appreciate, realize and ultimately leverage diversity of thought. Not to mention the ability to set aside egos and recognize our own blind spots (subconscious) that make it extremely challenging to see when true parity exists.

Here's an example: if you are sitting at a leadership table in your professional life and you take measure of those around you, only to find that most people sound like you, then diversity does not exist in that space. And by "sound" like you, I am being intentional. You see, it's the words that solve problems, not the looks. I have yet to see problems solved without words being muttered, typed or broadcasted. I have never seen telekinesis in action. Perhaps you will. No, it's the machinations of the brains of those with unique backgrounds that create new pathways to solve problems. They are evangelized to peers, leaders, friends, families and everything in between.

Your voice is an extremely powerful device. With its power, it can be used for both good and bad results. Hitler had a resounding voice but used it for ill-gotten gains. Martin Luther King Jr. had a voice that made angels pause, and he used it to inspire. Your mouth is important. It takes a distant back seat, however, to your ears. By being a truly active, engaged and deep listener, you will learn. If you learn, you become more aware. And, by becoming more aware, you can bring more of the variables into play when solving problems. If you aren't a great listener, you will never leverage diversity of thought.

Keep in mind: not everyone in the room can be right. Not everyone in the room can be wrong. The answer, however, still lies somewhere in that room. If it doesn't, you have either invited the wrong people (people who think like you) or, you need a bigger room. Be more inclusive to those who are willing to learn with their ideas, and experiences and you will see magic happen right in front of you. Learn and embrace the difference between inherent diversity vs. acquired. There's magic in each, but you must rinse it out and soak it into your brain.

P.S. We'll discuss in detail the Ladder of Inference and how our "biased" thoughts turn into actions.

"Diversity: the art of

thinking independently

together."

—Malcolm Forbes

Note
13

Don't Become an Ideologue Without Being Fully Informed

Earlier, I spoke of humility (and will continue to, by the way, so get used to it). It is one of the most powerful human characteristics.

If you are humble, you are a listener. If you are a listener, you can become a learner. A learner solves problems rather than creating them. Whenever I see someone so consumed with one side of an argument, I know rationalization will be hard to come by.

Growing up, I loved seesaws. Although I didn't recognize it at the time, there was a rhythmic ballet of compromise happening between my partner and me. We both knew that at some point, the other person had to push off the ground in order to continue this duet performance. An equilibrium wasn't necessarily the goal, but no one truly sought a disadvantage. Sure, if the other party possessed enough mass, then it became difficult to keep up. Being in sync though, by most people's standards, was the objective. What I liked most about the seesaw was the ever-changing point of view. When you went up, you saw the world differently. It consisted mostly of grass, trees, squirrels and of course your partner staring up at you (hopefully beaming with glee). When you went to the ground, you saw the sky, tops of trees, leaves, the occasional bird or butterfly, and of course your partner gazing down at you (still with glee unless there is a heights issue involved). This was truly my first experience seeing various points of view.

Take a magazine article you just read. After you finish it, you probably have fashioned an opinion on the matter. How did you come by this opinion? There are only two ways. The first is that the author framed it for you with the data you just consumed. The second is that you placed your personal experience into the story and came to a conclusion based on your own perceptions. So what's wrong with that? You've at least two points of view here, right? True . . . but let's talk motivations.

What did the author get out of writing the article? Was she paid to write it? If so, who paid her to write it? It's not to say that getting paid for a piece is wrong. Not at all. After all, 97 percent of the population gets compensated to do what we hope is a value-added job. And, it may be there is no ill intent whatsoever from the article. Just know, though, that unconscious bias is always in play. Those deep and innate biases in us cause judgment to occur without all the facts. The more voices you hear, the more data you gather, the more patience you apply to making informed decisions, the more likely a positive outcome will occur. We'll expand a bit more with Note 21 on cognitive dissonance.

"To find yourself,

think for yourself."

—Socrates

Note
14

Your Parents Will Make Mistakes; Jot Them Down and Reference Them Later

Your mother and I are far from perfect. We will raise our voices when we shouldn't.

We will accuse you wrongfully of leaving the dishes in the sink. We will overreact when you come home five minutes past curfew. We will not praise you enough for bringing home an excellent test score. We will not model the way by making our beds every day the way we should. Know these things will happen and that we will do our darndest to make sure we recognize them in real time and move to the next right action to correct them. These mistakes do not mean we love you any less. They happen because we love you so much. I know this is an adverse way of showing it, and this is why we will move through the mistake quickly and learn astutely (hopefully) from our failures. We hope to minimize them, of course, but take away some coaching nonetheless.

One of the best teachers I ever had was the worst leader I ever worked for. I made a note of so many practices that I would never emulate in my leadership role. This person was inauthentic, refused to honor commitments as if the refusal itself were a badge of honor and leaked narcissism as he glided across the floor. I'm fairly certain he believed he walked on water. I hold no ill will or indignation toward him. As a matter of fact, the experience was priceless. It was a doctorate of dictatorship, and this type of leadership was for short-term spurts with no chance of sustainability.

I prefer sustainability in many things: life, freedom, love, respect, impact . . . I could go on. Sustainability is a good word. We will, however, also be sustainable with our mistake-making. Together, we will keep each other honest with those mistakes and move through them.

"I've never made a mistake.

I've only learned from experience."

—Thomas Edison

Note
15

Nothing Is Taboo

I've seen and experienced too much in this world to label any subject too tough to talk about.

Whether it be death, sex, sexual preference, financial challenges, politics, religion or why UK fans truly dislike Duke (sorry, Honey), no subject is off the table. Getting uncomfortable means getting to a new place mentally. And this is always a grand thing to achieve.

Will your mother and I be perfect when it comes to these talks? Absolutely not. We will not, however, be dishonest with you. We may not have the right words, but they will be pure and reflect our opinions and experiences. It doesn't mean we are right; it's just what we have inferred over the years.

You, as an individual, must decipher the data we deliver and decide what you will take from it. At the core, I am asking you to trust us. Trust is not intangible. It is realized over time and experiences together. Trust is built through honoring commitments and lending advice with the purest of intentions. Trust is intuited from the core of who you are. Not everyone is wired to have this mindset and that is unfortunate. When you go right at a subject with no tap dancing, life becomes more efficient.

As Note 2 suggests, every day counts. Let's honor that by attacking difficult subjects head-on and working through them to resolutions. A resolution doesn't mean a win/win; it just means all voices were heard, acknowledged and appreciated. Taboo does not exist unless you let it. Squeeze this out of your vocabulary and your life will see better days because of it.

"When you are raised to think anything to do with sex is forbidden and taboo, then of course that's all you want to know about. That becomes your complete and utter fascination. That is the surest way to interest a child."

—Madonna

Note
16

Father vs. Dad

I don't believe these are mutually exclusive from one another. I see these as two different hats that a man can wear at the same time or separately.

Make no mistake, though, they are different in connotation.

As a father, I am looking out for your well-being. Are you safe? Are you aware? Are you street smart? Are you well-nourished? Are you making data-based decisions? As a father, I am in my rational state of mind. I am functioning consciously inside my brain's prefrontal cortex. This is where data is processed and non-fiction books live. I am sane, present and pragmatic with how I am thinking about my son.

As a dad, I am living more in the limbic part of my brain. Primarily, in the amygdala. This is where my emotions lie dormant until activated by an event. For example, if you came home intoxicated and I found out you drove home, I will most assuredly react emotionally and speak (incoherently) from the limbic portion of my brain. I will be erratic. If, however, it is 2:00 p.m. and you want to discuss politics, I will talk pragmatically from my neocortex. Just prepare yourself though, son. Most people talk politics from their amygdala. They are not rational on the topic. I, however, very much look forward to those discussions with you. Voting is not just a right; it is an obligation. As I mentioned in Note 13, by becoming informed you stay away from becoming a rigid ideologue. This allows you to make informed decisions. I digress.

I see the father/dad hats as mutual inhabitants in the home of a son. The key for me will be in knowing which hat to wear and when. I will not be perfect, but I do commit to being present. Challenge me when I'm wearing the wrong hat. I so appreciate healthy disagreements. The key word being . . . healthy. Just as I mentioned in "Diversity of Thought" the best resolutions come during juxtaposed points of view. Just as long as we are both talking from our prefrontal cortices, of course . . .

"A father is a man who expects his son to be as good a man as he meant to be."

—Frank A. Clark

Note
17

Selfishly
Selfless

This one pushes the valence of many people. That is certainly not my intent. It's the best way I have been able to describe investing in others.

If you are ever involved in leading others, professionally or personally, there will be a time when you reach a tipping point. A time in which the intrinsic value of mentoring, coaching or influencing others surpasses the extrinsic value you are receiving for the same act. Sounds selfless, doesn't it? Giving oneself for the betterment of a colleague, peer, friend or modest acquaintance. It is. But what happens when you do it with the full knowledge that through their gains, you will win? Through their upskills, you yourself will benefit. The time invested in them is really time invested in yourself. The reality is the more you do this, the more it is consuming. Dare I say it's addictive.

I was two stops away from my initial "corporate job" when I became a "one-man" band brokering real estate transactions needing financing. All I needed was a laptop and a phone to do the job. To say this was unfulfilling would be an understatement. My conundrum was simple: I missed coaching and mentoring others. I am by no means the best coach or the perfect mentor. Far from it. However, through my mistakes, I can make amends. Through my miscalculations, I can teach awareness to others. Through my non-risk-averse actions, I can share my learnings. In doing so, I feel rewarded.

Individual rewards by themselves are selfish. Think about it. Did Michael Phelps (trust me, you'll know this name) win all those golds by himself? Did he not have a coach, supportive parents, friends and teammates who willed him on? Make no mistake, he still had to put in the work. He earned those medals. What's next after a medal, though? I suppose you could say another one. This tactic may work for a short period of time. However, Mother Nature made sure this would not be a long-term sustainable strategy. Age always wins.

Is it wrong to be selfishly selfless? I don't believe it is. I feel it's important to go into it with your eyes wide open. It's important for both sides to know each other's motivations. In business, if you become known as a developer of others, you yourself will be recognized and most likely rewarded with a promotion or a merit increase. Is it selfish of you to accept? Not at all. It would be selfish of you not to. Your family would benefit from an enhanced financial position.

Invest in others and reap the intrinsic rewards that will surely follow. Dedicate yourself to a worthy cause and the boomerang of graciousness will gently hit you in the face. It will spike your dopamine levels in a much more practical (and healthy) way than illicit drugs. That's a whole other conversation . . .

"It's very true that you can be both selfless and selfish at the same time. What we tend towards, particularly in filmmaking, is this binary sort of, 'This is a good guy, this is a bad guy.' And I quite like the fact that life is a bit more complex than that."

—Hugh Grant

Note
18

Once You Post, It's Out There Forever

In the immortal words of football coach Herm Edwards, "Don't press send." He used to make this comment to rookie football players.

Why the warning? Once you post on a social media site, send an SMS text or email or drop a verbal line to someone who may be recording the conversation, it's too late to retract it. Think long and hard before you send that message. Think about the unintended consequences. Constituents you haven't thought of may hear the message.

I have a Rule of Three I like to use. I implemented it years ago when yours truly sent one of those emails I wished I could have retracted. If at least three people are going to see the message, you need to use this process. The process itself is quite simple. Read the email/SMS/tweet/post two times in your mind and then once out loud before sending. Your mind can catch things your voice can't, and vice versa. I'm amazed at how often I will change a message once I hear it out loud. The tonality could be causing an issue or just the way it comes off could be a completely different slant than intended. Remember to H.A.L.T. here as well. Don't make a decision or communicate a publicly focused message while in one of those states of being.

If ever in doubt, send the message to a trusted friend or colleague prior to posting. Sometimes, that deliberate delay can create a much-needed pause that can save you from embarrassment down the road. Don't let one communication define you. It's not to say you can't overcome it, but it will be an energy suck to do so.

"Not every part of your private life needs to be public."

—Author Unknown

Note
19

Financial
Literacy

Earlier, I mentioned FICO. Having a high FICO score is not financial literacy. It may show responsibility, but not literacy.

It simply means you pay your debts in a timely fashion and never let your debt-to-income ratio increase to an extreme level. Knowing how to balance your checkbook is not financial literacy. It just means you are decent at rudimentary accounting. Hiring a financial planner is not financial literacy. It means you are outsourcing the decision-making process for where to allocate your disposable income. What is disposable income? Income you can afford to part with. Financial literacy is not buying a home at the current market price and hoping for appreciation to occur over the long term. This is a gamble and thus not literacy. Financial literacy is not diversifying your paper assets into a mutual fund. You are then paying more fees (most likely after taxes) to invest in small returns.

Financial literacy is the understanding of how money really works and how to make it work for you vs. the other way around.

Financial literacy is more important than traditional education. It starts with the vernacular of money.

Assets = Income producing entities: rental homes (passive income), paper assets (portfolio income), businesses (you own vs. run).

Liabilities = Income deducting entities: primary home, cars, jewelry, clothes, season tickets for the local sports team, trips, nice dinners and fine wine. (Personally, I like to think of this one as an experience asset).

Expenses = These come from the liabilities list, plus many others. Most are avoidable or at a minimum controllable.

Cash Flow = Your total income – expenses = net cash (hopefully positive).

Rebalancing = The process of maintaining your target asset allocation. This helps to mitigate your risk of an off-kilter investment ratio.

Dollar Cost Averaging = Sometimes known as the "constant dollar plan." Contribute the same amount at the same cadences to reduce market volatility impact.

Marginal Tax Calculation = The real amount you pay when you increase your income threshold. (Ignore those pundits that say "Don't make more money, you'll pay more taxes!" It's rubbish.)

It took a financial nuclear bomb (2008 global recession) for me to realize my financial vernacular was less than sufficient. It was downright pathetic. You see, I thought the word "appreciation" was a financial term. And indeed, it is. It fits perfectly with Note 11. "I hope real estate goes up so I can refinance and cash out." I have one word to describe this phrase . . . ignorant. And that's what I was in 2008. I have been committed to my financial education ever since. To say I will never miscalculate an investment again would be a fool's statement. To say that the math will be methodical, deliberate, researched and without emotion, however, will be irrefutable. Here's a fun exercise. Take a penny and double it every day for thirty days and see what you get. Surprised? This is the power of compounding. We'll talk more about that . . .

> "An investment in knowledge pays
> the best interest."
>
> —Benjamin Franklin

Note
20

Psychology vs. Physiology:
Different yet Dynamically
Relevant

Most people believe behavior is rooted in psychology. In actuality, our behavior is a direct result of our physiology.

To be more direct, behavior is truly biology. The two major portions of your brain that shape decision-making are the neocortex and limbic systems. The limbic system is where your emotions rise. Think about H.A.L.T. Remember the feelings of anger and loneliness? The origins of these emotions are derived from your limbic system, specifically your amygdala. When you hear someone say, "I believe" or "I feel like," this is a qualitative response coming from this part of their brain. The neocortex is the more thoughtful/analytical part of the brain. When someone says, "The data doesn't lie" or "The results of the practice came from the daily execution of the fundamentals," the person is speaking from the neocortex. They are speaking quantitatively.

Think facts vs. feelings. Practical vs. perception. Realist vs. romantic. The limbic part of our brain does not focus on language. This is why it is difficult for us to compose a thorough response while experiencing a state of high emotion. Maslow's hierarchy of needs has a foundation of physiology before moving up sequentially-based psychological states and ending with self-actualization. We can have a full day conversation on this topic alone.

Physiology can also impact psychology in your daily discipline. For example, when you work out (lift weights or run), your body releases certain endorphins that invoke not only a euphoric feeling but also clarity of mind. Some of my better thoughts (yep, I do get those occasionally, son) have come during or after a workout. And even though my body doesn't take orders from me like it used to, I still work out every day. It's the energy that I otherwise could not achieve. It is my caffeine (as well as a cup of coffee . . . or two).

"Physiology and psychology cover, between them, the field of vital phenomena; they deal with the facts of life at large, and in particular with the facts of human life."

—Wilhelm Wundt

Note
21

Cognitive Dissonance

CD is the concept of holding two or more beliefs in your head that may be contradicting.

For example, a person may be an avid wine drinker (present company excluded, of course). Thought 1: I like to drink wine. Thought 2: wine could be bad for my health. How can one reconcile the two divergent thoughts? Another example would be if I am a Republican (I'm an Independent, by the way) and I decided to run for public office as a Democrat. This is dissonance. How could I possibly do this? More importantly, why am I even bringing up this topic? Simple. Just like diversity of thought brings the greatest solutions, so too does your ability to juggle two thoughts that equal a complete juxtaposition. This allows you to see multiple sides of the argument without a conscious bias. You already have a subconscious bias in play, and that is unavoidable.

As I mentioned in the intro, achieving self-actualization enables you to navigate the bias path. Having the ability to do this will positively impact your life. Whether or not it involves a disagreement with your spouse, a complex work problem, a debate on politics or religion or simply negotiating at your local town hall meeting, this ability can change the outcome to the positive. That's not to say a positive outcome translates into what may be considered a victory for you. It could translate into a pivot of your stance. It could lead to a win/win for multiple parties. It could reframe the next right action for a larger audience.

In the end, just be malleable when it comes to thoughts, not impregnable, but much more difficult. This does not apply to bedrock beliefs such as core values or tenets; those are cemented and should be hard to chisel away. By being humble and listening to diverse thinkers, you may even experience subtle movement on those foundational values.

> "Wisdom is tolerance of
>
> cognitive dissonance."
>
> —Robert Thurman

Note
22

Never Stop Learning . . . and Applying

Your brain is a data processor. It craves information. Your job is to feed it. Much like gas to a car, knowledge is to our brains.

You may not ever use all of it, but you'll be surprised by the retrieval power of your mind. Whether it be articles, books, TED Talks, mentors, school, friends, family, teachers or just plain observations, continue to learn about the world and the people in it. We are a fascinating species to study. And if you're bored of Homo sapiens, then study animals, the oceans, the stars or who knows what. By the time you turn thirty, perhaps we will have found some new alien friends with which to dine. The point is to never stop working out your mind. It will keep you sharp and relevant.

That's only half the equation. The other half is applying what you've learned. Knowledge is not power. It's the appropriate execution of that knowledge that translates into meaningful impact. As a side note, I loathe the word power. It smells of arrogance, egoism and hierarchy. In the context of leadership, people don't follow power; they follow authentically wired humble servants that honor their commitments (remember Note 1?). Use your learning to solve problems, offer advice, become an even better listener, invest your money, advance in your career, become a better partner and whatever else you deem necessary.

The point is to take action on your investment. It doesn't have to be immediate. We don't take action for the sake of it, but always with purpose. It doesn't mean it will always be the right action. Lord knows I've taken plenty of missteps in my life because I thought I was taking the right action. Lean into the failure, experience the pain of it, learn from it and move on. Such is the reflexive loop of decision-making. The difficulty will not be in giving in to rinse, cycle and repeat. You'll need a mechanism that automatically inserts itself into learning.

"Once you stop learning,

you start dying."

—Albert Einstein

Note

23

Once a Man,
Twice a Child

This is the wisest quote I ever received from my maternal grandfather.

When he first said it to me, I was under ten years old, so it didn't really register with me. It wasn't until he acquired Alzheimer's and deteriorated at a rather alarming rate that it grabbed ahold of my heart and mind.

When you enter this world, you will be entirely dependent upon your mother and me. When you leave this world, you will most likely be dependent upon someone else. As a child, your mind is without experience. As you grow into your senior years, your mind begins to experience less capacity, which is nearly synonymous with your formative years as a child. Your mother and I are committed to not placing the burden of taking care of us on your shoulders. From a financial, mental and health perspective, we are planning our final days to be independent of our children (yes, we are hoping you come with a bonus sister). Don't get me wrong, we want a ton of visits from you, letters, calls, emails, Zooms, Skypes, Holograms and frankly any other methods that connect us with you. It's just that we don't want to slap you with the "caretaker" tag. This is not a burden you will bear. Just know that our faculties will leave us at some point. We are just trying to evade this eventuality for as long as possible.

"Love your parents. We are so busy growing up that we forget they are growing old."

—Author Unknown

Note

24

When in Doubt, Be Nice

People will frustrate you. People will disappoint you. People will negatively surprise you. People will undermine you.

People will not honor commitments they make to you. People will cut you off in bumper-to-bumper traffic. People will yell at you. All this does not matter in the least. What does matter is how you respond. So when you feel like lashing out, retaliating, flipping the bird (yep, that still plays today), displaying condescending behavior or implementing passive aggression, just create a "power pause" and let your next action be that of kindness. At minimum, land back into equanimity. At maximum, just be nice.

It's amazing how disarming a warm smile can be. It's encouraging to see the exaltation that occurs when a positive word or tone reverses a disputatious conversation. It's mind-blowing how a simple wave to a terse driver can unconsciously cause them to take a few mph off their current course. Taking the high road is never easy. I'd relate it to taking the high ground in a battle. It's difficult to achieve, but becomes a strategic imperative.

I was visiting a company in Dubai that specialized in coaching change management to large corporations. They had many credos, but the beginning and most powerful one was the simplest: BE NICE. We discussed the internal civil war occurring between the limbic and prefrontal cortex portions of our brains. The amygdala is coaxing us to lash out and our prefrontal lobe is trying to be rational. Typically the yeller wins.

I am asking you to be mindful of the situation and your own internal fight-or-flight mechanism, and take the harder action. Take the action most will not. Take the high road and be nice. You'll find your intrinsic needs become much more satiated in both the short and long term. You'll find your blood pressure remains at a healthy level and your serotonin (sometimes called the happy chemical) breaches its reservoirs. Grudges never even form, much less last, in this state.

Forgiveness is paramount to a life of levity, lavishness of your soul and learning of your fellow humankind. Almost all of us are born to be attracted to compassion. Sometimes, though, we need to consciously act to bring it out of us. Being nice is such an act . . .

"To err is to be human;

to forgive, divine."

—Alexander Pope

Note
25

Work Hard,
Think Harder . . .

The secret to fast cash finally revealed!!! I know, I know, I know... you've heard this before, probably over a thousand times.

Of those thousand about 10 percent were actually creative or inventive enough to get your attention. Of that 10 percent, about 10 percent actually **sounded** as if their pitch made sense. Of that 10 percent, you went ahead and purchased 10 percent of what you heard. Let's see, 10 percent of a thousand is a hundred, 10 percent of a hundred is ten, 10 percent of ten is one. Congratulations, you only purchased one scam (I mean money-making machine) out of a thousand!!!!

I am certain I'm not the only one who is tired of seeing the same thing. Seeing email after email all containing keywords such as "Secrets" or "Cash" or "Revealed." I will give credit where credit is due. Several creative schemes out there pull at our heartstrings. The most widely used themes of appeal are focused on our need for money and more time with our families. Others focus on sports cars, fancy vacations and other egoist material things. Others focus on our children. How could you not afford to give your kids the life you never had? What kind of a parent would I be if I don't shell out a couple of bucks to make millions?

I am here to blow the lid off this industry and expose it for what it is: a bridge to somewhere! That's right, you heard me. They will definitely lead to somewhere, but it may not be where you think. The company selling you this idea, breakthrough plan or new way to rebuild the wheel will absolutely be living the dreams they tell you that you can live. They will do so on your dime. In the meantime, your cash has left your pocketbook (or Apple Pay Wallet) and your wife or husband stares at you like you are an idiot. There you stand, having risked your savings on a two-bit scam artist that promises everything and delivers nothing. That sports car in the email belongs to the guy who just took your money.

Why do we fall for this time and time again? I have thought long and hard about this and have come up with three conclusions.

1) We are struggling and in search of a way out. When someone dangles a carrot (and some of these carrots appear to be very juicy), we want to bite it. This tends to be human nature.

2) It is in our DNA to not want to "miss the boat" on a money-making opportunity. Scarcity is a grand selling technique and these scammers use it for all it's worth. How would you like to find out that you missed out on Google's IPO? Wouldn't you have liked to have known that gold was going to spike up to $2,500 an ounce over the last year? We WANT to be in on the next big deal. Part of that is for the money and the other part is because we simply can't help it!

3) The initial cost is usually so low we weigh the risk vs. reward. Why wouldn't I invest $49.99 to make $10,000 a week? What do I have to lose?

Let me address all three of these. First, when times are tough, we are at our weakest. There is a reason why a shark waits for a fish to be wounded or in distress before consuming it as a meal. We become easy targets when our capital is depleted and we are trying to figure out how to make the next month's mortgage payment. Enter the e-book shark, duh-duh, duh-duh,

duh-duh . . . ! (That was the theme song from Jaws, by the way, one of my all-time favorite films.) Just $49.99 and in a few weeks, you'll **pay off** that mortgage and buy a boat for your new indoor aquarium on your five-acre ocean view lot comprised of a ten-thousand-square-foot mansion with a bedrock of gold bullion.

Second, to "make the boat" is always a gamble. You shouldn't gamble unless you have the money to lose. IPOs and commodities trading are risky businesses. If you don't know what you are doing, you will get slaughtered. I don't care how easy they make it seem.

Third, why would anyone ever sell a $10,000/ week idea for $49.99, $99.99 or even $599? If the idea were truly genuine, you should be able to sell that idea for four thousand times the profit it will bring you. Are there really that many philanthropists out there who want their fellow humankind to be successful? Hmmm, I find that difficult to believe. Now I want to prepare you for something. I am going to beat a dead horse and bring out one of the oldest adages in the history of our species. Are you ready? Even if you are not, I am going to say it anyway: "**if it sounds too good to be true, it is . . .**"

I must sound like Congress. Here I am babbling about what **doesn't** work instead of telling you what does. Forgive me, as I am very passionate about this subject, and I want you to understand there are ONLY two ways to make money (other than being an employee). I challenge anyone to think of any other way than the two I put out here today. If you think of a third way, then you will be a gazillionaire.

HOW TO CREATE MONEY!

1) **Solve A Problem** – Finding solutions to existing issues is the pathway to riches. Think of Post-it notes, Velcro, Kevlar and the first Ford motor car. All were original concepts that solved issues. Post-its help remind us, Velcro helps bind us, Kevlar helps protect us and the car got rid of our horse and buggy.

2) **Take someone else's idea of solving a problem and do it better** – Rechargeable batteries, the space shuttle, Google and flipping houses. All were previous solutions to problems but were enhanced by other people. Rechargeable batteries saved us from purchasing new ones all the time, the space shuttle got rid of the capsules and having

to splash in the ocean upon reentry, Google recognized a lucrative niche of searching on the web and house flippers recognized a need to rehab older properties to bring up the value of the neighborhood and sell for a profit.

Thousands of examples exist and I could take up volumes of paper and much of your time listing them all out. My point here is that money can ONLY be made from those two ways. Was that a thump I just heard as your heart hit the floor? On the contrary, you should feel relieved. There should be a wave of euphoria about you because now you can finally focus your efforts on either of these two ways of making money. You can ignore the next e-book that comes your way and promises millions in just weeks. You can hit delete on the next "Get Rich While You Sleep" gig that passes through your inbox. You can now ignore those 1–4 a.m. infomercials that promise health and happiness with no extra effort on your part.

The only way to make money in this world is to "work hard, think hard." It is simple and it is real. Anyone who says anything else is simply selling you something.

Why am I telling you this? I want this final note to open up your eyes, ears and instincts. There are false "business prophets" out there taking advantage of people. A deal has got to be win/win or it is not a deal. A deal involves two people gaining an edge. One person's edge may be observed as being stronger, but nonetheless, both parties must have an edge. A win/lose is not a deal; it is simply taking advantage of another human being.

Work hard, think harder is the only way to experience wealth fulfillment. It'll be up to you to determine what level of fulfillment you'll need in life. This is a personal decision that only you can make. Just keep your eyes open and trust your internal instincts in making decisions. And by all means, don't make a decision in H.A.L.T. status . . .

"Work hard. Think big.

Listen well."

—Ben Feldman

Epilogue

You are here . . . I saw you come out of your mom's belly, taken to the warmer and placed back on top of your mom's chest for immediate skin-to-skin. All of these notes went to the far recesses of my mind in that moment. For in that particular moment in time, the only note, the only thought that mattered, was a sensation like none I've ever felt. It was an endearment that I believed to be possible, but couldn't surmise what the truth actually turned out to be. New fathers would say this to me many times, but it truly is not something that can be orally expressed. It must be experienced to fully garner the magnitude of that moment.

You are my son and you have my unconditional love. I look forward to each minute, hour, day, week, month and year we have together. I will commit to being present for each of those. Even in our first nights together when sleep was a distant rumor, I was as present as I know how to be.

Your life is now in front of you. This world doesn't yet know you, but it will. In your own unique way, you will leave an imprint on it and those who inhabit it. I am so proud of you and yet we haven't even had a reciprocated conversation. You've already heard my singing, story and silent voices. I hope I haven't tormented you too much with my insufficient pipes. Early on, it looks like you and I will have some nice karaoke battles ahead of us.

I write this epilogue on Day Six of our union together. Today is Mother's Day. You should know your mother was a consummate warrior this past week. She reached deep into a reserve I did not realize she possessed. Not only did my love deepen even more for her, but so did my respect. You and I both got extremely lucky to have her in our lives. I am in awe of her ability and commitment to be the best mother and wife humanly possible.

Final note: Your path is your own. No one can tell you how to walk it. Not even us. Responsibility lies with you. You have our total aggregate love and support. Ignore the doom and gloom of our manufactured news. The world is truly what you make of it. You can give in or give it your all. That is your choice. I, for one, cannot wait to see your footprints on this life. Your legacy has begun.

There will be peaks and valleys, days to remember and those to forget. You will love, you will lose and you will triumph over the steepest of challenges thrown at you. We will be in your corner cheering the entire time. You will battle nothing alone. And there will be battles. Never stagnate in sorrow; keep moving forward. Don't fast forward to the future; instead, take a pause in the present. (I do this every time I look at you.) You have a life of your own to experience and you will make hundreds/thousands of mistakes just like I have. Learn and leave them in your rearview quickly. And each step of the way, for each victory and defeat you realize, your mother and I will be there taking notes. . .

Acknowledgments

Thank you to Polly for opening up these marketing virgin eyes. Thank you to Tasha Brown for your creative brilliance in the exterior design of this book. Thank you, Victoria Wolf, for the magic you conducted with the interior of this book. Jennifer Jas thank you for keeping the intent of my notes in tact while correcting my more than unacceptable grammatical errors. Thank you to my publisher, Andrea Constantine, for holding my hand throughout this process. I knew I had a lot to learn about publishing the book. You made my learning curve so much less daunting. Thank you to Russell Owens for teaching me Note 4 and the discipline to see this commitment through. Thank you to my mom and dad for putting your hearts and souls into raising your two sons. A lack of effort or will was never a concern for you. Thank you to Donna McCoy for catching the magic of me holding my son that first night in the hospital room. It's the same photo that resides on the back of this very book. Thank you, Jeff, for being an older brother I could always depend on to get my back. Thank you to my wife for being my bedside editor. Your patience so supersedes my own. For that and so many other reasons, I am grateful you said yes to walking the rest of this unpredictable road called life with me. Thank you to Summit. For without you, this book does not see the light of day. Lastly, thank you to all those who gave guidance to this new father. Even though I may not have heeded all of it, I was and always will be listening.

About the
Author

Eric Lynn spends his professional life managing workforce solutions for small, midsized and Fortune 1000 companies. With years of professional experience, Eric understands the value of preparation. Thus when his wife, Ashley, became pregnant, Eric sought a way to prepare for his new role as a father. Something shifted within him causing him to ask different questions of life.

As he awaited the arrival of his first child, future conversations with his son, Summit, began to take shape. Eager to prepare for this new role, *Notes to My Son* was born.

The Lynn family lives in Colorado where they enjoy climbing 14ers, skiing, playing tennis and appreciating the abundance of all nature has to offer. Eric and his family hope that the relatable life wisdom shared in this book touches the hearts of all who read it.

Visit his website at www.Notes2MySon.com.

Printed in Great Britain
by Amazon